From Numpty Diver
to MSD in six months!

From Numpty Diver
to MSD in six months!

Mel Close

Dedicated to my dad, Derek Sergeant,
who supported and encouraged me
in everything I did, including diving

Copyright © Mel Close, 2005

First published in 2005 by
Scotforth Books
Carnegie House
Chatsworth Road
Lancaster LA1 4SL
www.scotforthbooks.com

British Library Cataloguing-in-Publication data
A catalogue record for this book is available from the British Library

ISBN 1-904244-40-8

Printed by Alden Press

PADI – The Way the World Learns to Dive
OR
'From Numpty Diver to MSD in 6 months'!!

Discover Scuba

Tenerife:
Sun
Blue Sea
Tropical fish
Wetsuit
Warm water ...

Open Water Diver

2 Students
1 PADI Instructor
1 plastic table thing
4 pool sessions
1 Compass
1 Dry Suit (Hmm!)
4 Open water dives
100 mask skills and ... a million fin pivots! (Well it felt like it!!)

Advanced Open Water Diver

Deep Dive
Multilevel (a £37 plastic thing!)
Night (with fireworks!)
Navigation
Another compass
Another plastic thing
Another Dry Suit and more mask skills and more Fin Pivots!

Specialities

Enriched Air (3 pieces of plastic!)
DPV's (Great Fun, no finning)
Deep Underwater Naturalist (not in UK!) Navigation with Compass (I've come a long way!)

Rescue Diver

Book
Video
Exam
Knowledge Reviews
1 bank Holiday weekend
Loads of Bruises
Yet another plastic thing

MSD

Hurray, I can dive!

Glossary of Terms

BCD (Buoyancy Control Device) – the inflatable jacket that divers wear over their wet or drysuits. They can be inflated or deflated to adjust your buoyancy under the water or on the surface.

Instructor – teaches you everything you need to know to learn to dive, including mask skills and fin pivots – easily recognisable underwater by their handclapping and handshake signals.

DM (Divemaster) – a diver on the first rung of the 'professional ladder' – instead of doing mask skills and fin pivots they get to watch other people doing them instead!

Knowledge Reviews – found at the end of each chapter in every course manual. Have to be completed before the end of each course and are 'marked' by your instructor – anyone not getting a hundred percent on these is a numpty diver because the answers are all in the book!

Fins – are worn on the feet to enable you to move effortlessly when in the water, and make you walk like a duck on dry land!

Mask – self explanatory – you can't see underwater without it.

Fin Pivot – a 'skill' in many of the courses designed to help you 'fine tune' your buoyancy.

Capernwray – a disused quarry near Carnforth that has been turned into a dive site with a 'Underwater Theme Park'. This means there are 'attractions' such as boats, helicopters, planes etc under the water for you to look at. NB. This only seems odd the first time you see them down there!

PADI – Professional Association of Diving Instructors

DPV (Diver Propulsion Vehicles) – battery operated underwater scooters.

Eccleston Delph – another disused quarry, in Eccleston near Preston, that has been turned into a dive site. Underwater attractions include a van, cruiser, armoured car, sports car etc.

Recreational Dive Planner – the first dive tables designed for planning and making no decompression recreational dives.

Slate – a white piece of plastic that you write on with a special pencil, Usually attaches to your BCD.

Viz – visibility – how clear the water is and how far you can see. The main topic of conversation at dive sites.

Plastic wheel –the 'wheel' version of the recreational dive planner, allows you to plan multilevel dives.

Cylinders – sometimes known as 'tanks' – a cylindrical metal container used to safely store high pressure air so you will have something to breathe underwater. They come in a variety of capacities, the most common sizes are 10, 12 and 15 litres.

Sump – the deepest part of the quarry.

(A) Numpty Diver – as, 6 months ago, I couldn't swim very well, didn't like putting my face in the water and was crap at snorkelling let alone diving, I think this phrase described me very well.

(B) Master Scuba Diver (MSD) – this PADI rating is the highest 'non-professional' rating a diver can attain. The classification denotes 'superior achievement in diving' and, to achieve this rating, a diver must be a PADI Advanced Open Water Diver, a PADI Rescue Diver, hold 5 speciality certifications and show proof of 50 logged dives. I'm now one of these!

So ... how did I get from A–B in 6 months?
Good question! Here's my 'journey' . . .

Discover Scuba Try Dives

My daughter Natalie, my friend Judith and I did 4 Discover Scuba 'try dives' whilst on holiday in Tenerife and we loved them: beautiful blue skies, wetsuits, one to one instruction, someone to set our gear up, surface temperature 30 degrees, water temp 24 degrees, plenty of Aquatic life etc, etc, etc – Idyllic!

A 'Discover Scuba try dive' is an introductory session, either in the sea (abroad) or in a pool (in the UK) during which participants learn the basics of scuba diving and enjoy a short dive with an Instructor.

Feeding the fish on try dive

From Numpty Diver to MSD!

Judith on try dive

Natalie on try dive, Tenerife, August 2004

Open Water Diver (October 2004)

Full of enthusiasm from our try dives my friend and I signed up at Fins Watersports in Preston, for the PADI open water certification course, because we wanted to learn to dive, and diving in this country couldn't be that much different form diving abroad, could it?? This was also when I set myself my first goal – to be open water certified ready for my holiday in Tunisia on the 22nd October 2004.

The staff at the Fins shop had told us to be at 'Hutton Grammar School swimming pool' for 8pm on a Tuesday night in September. We arrived, via the main entrance (the wrong entrance!) early and spent the next half an hour, in the rain, looking for the pool and/or any signs of life. We looked round everywhere and couldn't work out why there where no other cars or people. Little did we know that there was another entrance, and we eventually found the pool and signs of life – our instructor (Dave Small) who, was genuinely pleased to see us, obviously he didn't know that we'd spent half an hour searching for the place and were in no mood to learn to dive – shame! I think we gave him a hard time – whoops, not a good start!

The PADI 'open water certification' qualifies you to dive independently to a maximum depth of 18 metres, procure air fills and scuba equipment and plan, conduct and log open water dives when equipped properly and accompanied by a buddy. As a full entry level qualification. It also allows you to continue your diver training with other PADI courses. In order to pass the course you have to successfully perform a number of skills during four confined (pool) sessions and 4 open water dives. In addition there is a manual to read with knowledge reviews at the end of each chapter that must be completed and then an exam.

Pool (Confined Water) Sessions

We got changed and went to the pool side where Dave was waiting for us – still apologising for us getting lost – even though it wasn't his fault – I think he could tell we weren't happy (don't know how!!).

We did, however, quite sensibly put our annoyance at getting lost to one side, and tried to stop being 'prickly' with our instructor, after all he was gonna teach us to dive – we were annoyed but we weren't stupid!

Admittedly the lesson got better and, like the rest of the confined water sessions we thoroughly enjoyed them, I'm not sure we ever stopped giving Dave a hard time though!

There are quite a lot of skills to learn during these sessions including; equipment assembly and disassembly, regulator recovery – that's where you learn how to recover it and put it back in your mouth underwater (this seemed quite scary but actually it was alright), alternate air source use, weight removal underwater and at the surface, controlled emergency swimming ascent (CESA) and how to remove cramp on yourself or your buddy. The swimming pool, or confined water, sessions are a safe place to learn and practise these and other skills that are essential for open water diving. I think my problem however, and maybe it's the same for all new divers was that, at the time, I couldn't see the relevance of the skills and why you have to keep practising them, as I had no diving experience and nothing to relate it too, this meant that my friend and I did maybe 'whinge' a bit when doing them. Fortunately our instructor kept stressing how important they were and made us keep practising till he was happy that we had mastered the skill, this was good (though I didn't think so at the time) because when it came to my open water dives and when I needed to use some of the skills (suddenly they were relevant) I remembered how to do them – thankfully!

There were moments, however, during the pool sessions, when I felt the instructor got his own back on us, moments like: 'Clear your mask underwater' – lets do it again, and again, and again; 'fin pivot' – lets do it again, and again, and again. Well yes, obviously I know they are part of the skill requirements for the course – but that many times?

Then there was the skill showing you how to 'exit from the water onto a boat' (well poolside actually) – we struggled with that one, literally, and couldn't see why someone couldn't just help us out onto the side of the pool; after all (as we kept pointing out) it wasn't like we'd actually ever be doing this in real life was it? Surely other people on the boat would help you out, or it would have steps! Whoops again! – me and my big mouth! "

We were also quite shocked and amazed to find that on pool session two (yes two) we, not our instructor or DM, were expected to set up our scuba gear – on our own!! We were OK to put it together but we didn't trust ourselves to actually use it afterwards, I mean what if we'd

Judith struggling out onto poolside

set it up wrong and it didn't work?! We got round this (every week actually) by casually saying "could you just check this please?" What we actually wanted to say was "My God, this is lifesaving equipment, shouldn't an instructor be doing this??" But out of all the times we asked someone to check, we hadn't once done it wrong – so we did know what we were doing, we just weren't very confident!

> **The term 'Scuba Gear' refers to the air cylinder, BCD, regulators and pressure gauges that are set up to create the 'Self Contained Underwater Breathing Unit'. A Buoyancy control Device (BCD) is an expandable bladder that you inflate or deflate to regulate your buoyancy. The most common is the jacket style, worn like a coat that holds your air cylinder in place as well as providing buoyancy control. A regulator enables you to breathe the air from the cylinder. It reduces the scuba tank's high pressure to match the surrounding water pressure. The first stage attaches to the tank valve and there is a second stage which has the mouthpiece on it.**

It was on these four pool sessions that we also learnt the standard hand signals that would ensure we could 'communicate' with our instructor and each other underwater – it was also at these sessions that my friend and I started to 'invent' our own hand signals that would enable us to communicate only with each other!

Within diving there are a lot of mnemonics to help you remember the sequence of events for things that need to be remembered in a particular order, such as buddy checks, descending and ascending. One of these is SORTED, which stands for Signal, Orientate, Regulator, Time, Elevate and Descend. These are drummed into you during training as they are so important – if you remember the mnemonic you

OK

remember the sequence of events to go with it. On one of our descents Judith and I, with Dave were going through the descending sequence but went from O to T, missing out the R – for regulator which is there to remind you to swop your snorkel for your regulator so you can actually breathe underwater, quite a vital one really. As we started to let the air out of our BCD's and descend Dave signalled to us, we came back up and he reminded us to put our regulators in. Had we descended much further we would soon have been coughing and spluttering as the water entered our snorkel. Were we eternally grateful and apologetic to Dave? No, we found it highly amusing and everyone had to wait for us to stop laughing before we could continue. However, neither of us have ever forgotten again!

The pool sessions were from 8pm till 9.15pm every week and then there was the de-brief, and knowledge reviews to go through in the pub afterwards. This could be quite tiring after having worked all day and, every week, on our way there, before the pool sessions, Judith and I would look at each other and say "means to an end, this is a means to an end" and after every pool session we would agree what fun we'd had! The sessions were hard work, as there was a lot to learn, but they were always fun.

Open Water Dives

Confined water sessions over, knowledge reviews completed and exam passed, we were ready and prepared for the open water sessions — yeah right!

Down to Fins we went to try on the gear and for our first experience of 'dry suits'. As I'm quite tall, I had to have a large one which meant the feet were 3 sizes too big — for every 2 steps my feet took, the boot moved one! My friend couldn't wear a dry suit, as the neck seal was far too tight (worried about her 'carotid' artery!), and so used a 7mm wetsuit.

> **The carotid arteries are in your neck and if your hood or dry suit neck seal is excessively tight it can compress these arteries. Your brain may then perceive this as high blood pressure and respond by slowing your heart down which can then cause you to faint. Fortunately this is very, rare and most people wear dry suits without any discomfort.**

Day One and we met at the Fins shop for 9am; we weren't really nervous as we didn't know what to expect, and we were also quite excited, back to real diving in the open water — just like Tenerife! (As new divers we were still quite naïve as well!) We had another student with us, Andy, who was also doing his open water certification at the same time — lucky him!

At the time I thought the staff in the shop were being kind when they made us a coffee — now I know it was because they knew what we had in store for the next two days, and felt sorry for us! The open water part of the course is nearly always held at Capernwray Dive Centre, near Carnforth, as it's an ideal site for training dives.

So off we went there on a cold October morning, someone should have warned us about the car park, and the fact that it would be full of overweight, half naked men getting changed into their dive gear – too much testosterone and bare flesh for that time on a Saturday morning!

Mind you, I did think that on a good day we might stand a chance of 'copping off', and having a romantic liason with some gorgeous diver. Hah! that was before I knew what we looked like when we came out of the water, with a face full of snot and having a bad hair day (no-one warned us about that either) Good job we were only interested in diving!

We were briefed, got kitted up and, after asking our instructor to check the gear (still didn't trust ourselves) we got changed and were ready for our first open water dive. It was only when we got to the waters edge that I noticed my friend and I looked slightly different to all the other divers – we were wearing bright, and I mean fluorescent bright, yellow hoods! Everyone else, ie every other diver in the quarry was wearing a black hood! When we asked why we had to wear yellow hoods, Dave told us it was Fins policy for students to wear yellow hoods so they could be easily identified under the water. That was a good answer, and a fair point, but a part of me still thought it was another one that was more for the instructors amusement. Mental note: first item of dive gear to buy should be a black hood!

We were also introduced to Bev, who would be doing our 'surface cover' for the weekend, this meant we had to give her details of where we would be going how much air we had and how long we were expected to be. She, in turn checked everyone as they came out of the water and logged how much air they had left. I was to find out later that Fins have someone doing this for every course, it reassures you knowing such procedures are in place and it means there is a none diver to look after keys, help you

Gearing up at Capernwray

with your suit etc. Bevs a real star at surface cover, and has subsequently done it for many of my courses, I can always rely on her to help me with anything from taking photo's, helping me into my suit, looking after my flask or just keeping my stress levels down!

Into the water and onto the dives. All I remember from the first dive, which was a dry suit orientation dive, was thinking "what the **** is going on with this dry suit?" I either felt shrink wrapped, was rapidly ascending and on my way up (just put your arm up to dump the air they said – like it was that easy!) or bouncing off the bottom! It was at this point I realised something else that everyone knew but had kindly neglected to tell me: diving in this country is nothing like diving abroad! My logbook entry for this dive says 'Dry suit v. dodgy – it shrink wraps you!!' that says it all really!

There are 2 main types of exposure suits that divers wear (dry suits and wet suits). Diving in the UK, particularly in winter, usually involves wearing a dry suit as they provide more insulation than a wet suit. The dry suit insulates you with a layer of air plus you usually wear a warm undergarment with it as well, this makes a noticeable difference in how long it takes you to feel cold and therefore means your dive time is longer. Dry suits fill with air directly from your cylinder via a low pressure inflator hose. This also means you have to put air into your suit when descending and remember to release expanding air as you ascend.

The next three dives, over two days, consisted of either doing mask skills (again and again!) or fin pivots (again and again!) with the odd 'hover' thrown in for good measure, and of being very cold – Oh, and we saw a boat an a couple of horses down there – not that I could look at them for too long as I was either too high up to see or trying to get off the bottom!

I still can't work out why instructors make us do the skills so many times but I suspect it's so they can practice their own skills – those underwater handshakes and handclapping!!

Dive four saw my first introduction to a compass, and the start of a six month long deep, psychological fear of them! I had to navigate (and I use the term loosely) a straight line and the reciprocal heading. Fortunately, for me, I did the skill with an assistant instructor who was acting DM for the day, he had the patience of a saint as I 'winged it' – whatever this 'navigation thing' was, I wasn't getting it! (Little did I know it was going to come back to haunt me at a later date.)

Also during our open water weekend was the numerous

Pe-dive briefing with instructor – in the car park

times we had to take our scuba gear off at the surface and put it back on, and again I remember giving Dave a hard time as I protested loudly, about being cold and asking why couldn't he help me because wasn't this was another 'skill' I was never going to need in real life? (another one that was going to come back to haunt me!)

There were also some very large 'trout' on the way back to our exit point – the last thing I needed when I was concentrating on not doing an uncontrolled ascent in that suit was a load of large fish getting in my way!!

However, both my friend and I passed and were given our 'temporary' certification card, which I flew off to Tunisia with 2 days later. First goal achieved.

Being presented with temporary certification

Judith being presented with temporary certification card

Tunisia (October 2004)

I took the opportunity, whilst on holiday in Tunisia to dive with a local company, they had the PADI logo up so I assumed they must be OK!!

We went out in a small (ish) boat and when we got to our dive site they inflated a BCD and threw the SCUBA gear over the side. I felt OK about this as it wasn't mine, which I had (very) carefully set up myself and kept one eye on it all the time we were in the boat. "That is yours Melanie" they said and pointed to the one in the water, rapidly floating away! Bugger! I didn't like to ask how I got out of the boat and into the water, I'd already noticed there were no steps, so I put on my mask and fins, put the snorkel in my mouth (as instructed a million times during training) and made a very unladylike and ungainly entrance into the sea and started chasing my gear. Once I caught up with it, I had flashbacks of Capernwray less than a week earlier, taking the gear off at the surface and putting it back on. I remembered all my protests to Dave, "why do we have to do it — again". Now I was bobbing about in the middle of the sea thinking 'shit, me and my big mouth, how did we do it'?

The dives were fine with plenty of marine life and good visibility, on one of the dives though I accidently put my hand on a sea urchin and the spines went into my fingers and one went straight down my thumb nail — ouch! On my holiday reps advice I visited the nearest chemist who then sent me to the local doctors, who, unfortunately, didn't speak any English. They took the spines out of my fingers and half of the one from under my thumbnail —

the other half was taken out at the Royal Preston Hospital on my return from holiday. Why, you might ask, did I only have half taken out in Tunisia? No anaesthetic − enough said, there's only so much pain you can take!

It also became apparent early on that as a certified diver I was expected to be self sufficient, I buddy checked myself as no-one else was going to do it and I was left on my own at 20m to swim around without a 'buddy' for 15 minutes. Fortunately, as I now acknowledge, I had been well trained, and I remembered everything I had to do to have a safe and enjoyable dive − maybe all those skills were for a good reason after all!

> **During the open water course you are trained in the 'Buddy System' ie, always dive with a buddy who stays close by at all times. Your buddy assists you with things like putting your equipment on, checking it before you dive, they can also remind you to check your depth, time and air supply limits and, in the unlikely event of an incident they provide emergency assistance. And, obviously, you do the same for your buddy. A proper buddy system is essential to safe, fun diving.**

After the dive, the boat came to pick us up last, everyone else was already in it and they expected me to climb in, on my own! Oh No, momentary panic when I realised how high out of the water the sides of a boat actually were! (Why don't they have steps?) After struggling for what seemed like ages, not helped by me finding it hilarious as well, I looked into the boat to see my daughter, Natalie, sat there laughing at me! I asked how she had got in and she said "I just held out my arms and two of them pulled me in − easy" − so I held out my arms and ... they shouted "hurry up, we need to get back to

In a wetsuit - must be abroad!

shore" – great!" They didn't seem to find it as funny as I did either. In the end I had to stand on my buddy's shoulders to get in (nearly drowning him), and even then I still struggled. Another flashback: confined water (pool) session number 3, and oh my gosh, you do use the skills in real life, and yes, they are for a good reason – sorry Dave, I take it all back!!

I also realised that having the PADI logo up does not mean that a dive school is a registered PADI centre; this dive school wasn't registered, they just had a variety of PADI publicity materials on display. Another mental note: check future dive schools on PADI website to ensure they are registered.

Advanced Open Water Course (November 2004)

I knew that if I was continue diving in this country, which I really wanted to do, that I would have to 'learn to love' (and properly control) my drysuit. Diving in Tunisia had also shown me that the open water certification was just the start of it; I had a lot more to learn! Fortunately PADI had plenty of courses to enable me to do so!

Back to Fins to book the Advanced Course (Lucky Dave!!), which was to be goal number 2. I had already decided which 3 dives I wanted to do – Dry Suit (had to be), Night and Multilevel, then there were the two mandatory dives, Deep and Navigation (oh no, that again!!). I also decided to do the Enriched Air speciality at the same time. This meant I had two manuals to read, lots of knowledge reviews to complete and 2 exams to do! However, on the positive side I got loads of plastic tables including a very complicated looking £37 plastic wheel, for the multilevel! At least I'll never have problems defrosting the freezer again!

The advanced open water certification consists of doing 5 'adventure dives'. Each dive introduces you to the basics of different underwater activities/topics. It's a great way to find out what particular type of diving interests you, for example wreck diving, night diving etc. If you make 5 different adventure dives in deep, navigation and 3 others you then become an 'advanced open water diver' and can dive to 30 metres.

Outside Fins with Cushla after booking another course

Having read the manuals (cover to cover obviously), completed the knowledge reviews (without looking up the answers obviously) and passed the 2 exams (obviously), I was ready to do my 5 dives.

First up was my night dive, this was done on the 5th November (Bonfire Night) at Capernwray. It was also their 10th Birthday and they were throwing a bit of a party with free entry, food and fireworks. Now I'm not saying that divers are fickle but it was packed, on a cold Wednesday night in November, nothing to do of course, with the free diving, food and fireworks. Yeah right!

Not only was it crowded and dark but the viz was really bad as well, and it was the first time I had used a torch underwater!

The dive was OK, with only one dodgy skill — switching the torches off — I switched mine off and froze like a statue cos I figured the dark wasn't a problem as long I didn't move, not even an inch! I was also desperately hoping that no-one else moved either! No mask skills though, or fin pivots – hurray!

Next up was the dry suit dive, this taught me more about how the suit worked, how to dump air when ascending, what to do if the valve stuck etc. It also made me more confident as I understood more about how the suit worked. My buoyancy was also getting better so I found the dive less stressful, and ... we were back on familiar territory ... fin pivots and hovers! Better the devil you know!

I did the dive on enriched air for the speciality; didn't notice any difference though, except that I had to 'verify' the content using a little gadget!

Enriched air nitrox is the latest tool in a divers efforts to stay underwater for longer. Enriched air replaces some of the nitrogen in the air with oxygen. This means that you absorb less nitrogen during a dive which, in turn, gives you longer no decompression limits. The PADI Enriched Air Course teaches you the procedures for no decompression diving with enriched air nitrox. You also learn how to use enriched air dive computers and tables for planning dives within no stop limits and oxygen exposure limits. You also learn about the special issues related to the equipment used with enriched air. Before each dive the diver must personally verify the oxygen content using an oxygen analyser.

After I had finished the dives and got changed I went to have a look round the dive shop at Capernwray. I was fascinated by the wide variety of dive gear available as it was all still so new to me – and I didn't know what half of it was for! What really caught my eye though was an 'underwater notebook'! Now, I had kind of got used to writing on the white plastic slates underwater with the special pencil, but an underwater notebook, I couldn't get my head round this – paper that you can write on underwater? Didn't seem quite right really did it? And why would you need it, what do divers do down there that they would need a notebook for? Write their shopping list? take notes on what the fish are doing?

So, I had a quick look round the shop to make sure no-one was watching me and I had a quick feel at the paper – I had to know if it was 'real' paper! And it was, it felt just like real paper anyway, so I'm still quite fascinated by it. However, as it cost almost fifteen pounds I didn't buy one, I wasn't that fascinated.

Dive 3 was my 'navigation' dive. My logbook for this dive says 'Great Fun' – Hmm ... that covers a multitude!'

As you may remember the navigation bit of my open water dives did not go well, and this was in my mind as I walked round Capernwray car park with compass in hand and Dave's coat over my head to practice using the compass. (Now tell me thats not for the instructor's amusement only!!).

I did the customary square, without using the compass really, as I still hadn't grasped how to use it properly, and I couldn't see it under the coat anyway.

During the dive the square had to be repeated underwater. But, I had a plan as to how I was going to 'wing' this one! I had already learned that from a start point of 90 degrees the turns would be 180, 270 and 360, and I had these memorised, ready to write in the appropriate place on my navigation slate so it would at least look like I knew what I was doing.

So, I was knelt on the bottom slate in hand, ready to go and Dave wrote **140** degrees on it – aargh! So I promptly rubbed it out and wrote 90

Compass practice

– it had to be 90, I couldn't do any other! You can tell I still wasn't getting it!

The look on Dave's face when I changed it was an absolute picture – but he wasn't having it and promptly rubbed it out and re-wrote 140 degrees, bugger! So I had to set off, I managed a square of sorts, we had to stop though to have a 'discussion' when I was writing the numbers on my slate as 'one of us' couldn't add up!

For the 'natural navigation' skill I knew, from the briefing, that we were to swim out with the wall on our left, stop, turn and I was to take us 'home'. So, Dave gave the signal that we were doing this bit and we set off with the wall on our left, I was quietly confident about this skill as all I had to do was turn round and swim back – even I couldn't get that wrong could I? Dave then stopped us and gave me the signal to take us home. At this point I need to tell you that what Dave meant was take us right back home, as in back to the exit point and out of the water.

However, I thought he meant take us back home as in back to the rock where we had started the skill!

I turned around and took us right back to the large rock where we had started the skill, feeling quite pleased with myself I looked at Dave who signalled 'No'. Thinking it was the wrong rock I swam on to the next one and looked at him again. He was frowning and shaking his head at me and signalled 'No' again! So, I swam to the next rock — his next signal was somewhat different from the others, but I got the message! An underwater 'debate', with a variety of hand signals ensued which ended with us all swimming back 'home' together. Obviously just a slight misunderstanding!

Multilevel diving enables you to plan profiles that credit you for slower nitrogen absorption when you ascend to a shallower depth. This provides more no-stop dive time. The 'wheel version' of the recreational dive planner is used to plan the dives.

The Multilevel dive, Number 4, was good because most of the skills were done beforehand and were more about planning the dive and learning to use the wheel (plastic thing). Then all I had to do was dive what I'd planned. This was great because after the navigation dive I needed a nice, easy, straightforward one!

The last dive for my advanced certification was the deep dive. Well, as deep as you can get in a quarry. I managed almost 21 metres at the sump by almost burying my arm in the silt! I could have got 22 but I wasn't prepared to go up to the elbow – it stirs up the bottom and buggers up the visibility too much!

That done, I had passed them all and received the Advanced certification and my first speciality – the Enriched Air. But ... did it make me love my dry suit and motivate me to keep diving in this country??

Well, I have to say, yes it did. By the time I had completed my Advanced, the combination of gaining additional information through the manual and knowledge reviews, Instructor briefings and then the actual dives meant I was a better, more confident diver and, although I still can't say I love my dry suit, we do get on a lot better now!

I had also achieved goal number 2 and now needed to set number 3 – I decided to try and get from 'Numpty Diver' to MSD in 6 months. This meant I had to do the rescue diver course, 4 more specialities and another 40 or so dives before the end of April (ish)! This goal definitely felt a bit too ambitious – but I could try!

I knew that to get the 40 dives logged before the end of April that I was going to have to dive a lot in the UK during the winter months – brr!! As I was off work for two weeks over the Christmas period I took the opportunity to get in some pleasure dives during this time. One of these was at Capernwray on the 5th January, the water temperature was 7 degrees for this dive, as it was for most of the ones I did during Xmas and New Year – very refreshing! The dive was with Dave Small and we had agreed that towards the end of the dive I could have a try at using his DSMB (Delayed Surface Marker Buoy). This is a long, brightly coloured inflatable tube that attaches to a reel, the idea is that you inflate it with air when underwater, it then goes up to the surface so a boat or other divers know where you are, and you can then reel in the line as you ascend.

We had a good dive and at the end of it stopped at

around 8 metres at the 'Dreamer', one of the sunken boats. Dave unhooked the DSMB from his BCD (where else) and handed it to me, we'd gone through how to use it whilst on the surface, so I took it off him and got ready to use my alternate air source to put just a bit of air into it. I knew I didn't need very much, just enough to start it ascending, as it went up the air in it would expand and fill it up. I unravelled some of the line and put a bit of air into it, I wasn't ready though for how fast the air would expand and I had to grab onto the boat as I almost went up with it!!

Then, when I had to reel the line in, I got very fed up as my arms were aching — I didn't realise that 8 metres of water, and therefore 8 metres of line would be that difficult and tiring to reel in! That was my first, and last for a long time, experience of delayed surface marker buoys! Another mental note: if I need to use one when diving get my buddy to do the reeling in bit!

Specialities (November 2004–April 2005)
Enriched Air (November 2004)

Done in conjunction with the Advanced, see above.

The next three specialities were all done whilst on holiday in Tenerife. The diving there was great (and I was back in a wetsuit) however there were some problems. My instructor was insistent that he knew how much weight I should need and wouldn't let me do a buoyancy check or use any more weight, telling me I should be able to use just my lungs to adjust the buoyancy! He gave me 4kg for all dives except the DPV (Diver Propulsion Vehicles) ones which he gave me none for! His logic was that the DPV weighs 2kg so I wouldn't need any, this meant effectively that I had gone from the 6–8kg I would normally use to 2kg, as long as I kept hold of the DPV, none if I let go of it! Didn't seem very logical to me, and was a constant source of heated debate between me, other students and the instructor throughout our holiday.

I think I 'irritated' them a bit as well, by keep asking about things like buddy checks, safety stops, buoyancy checks etc- not a lot to ask for! There was me thinking that all dive schools and instructors used the same standards and procedures – how wrong can you be!

It's very important, in diving, to be able to control your buoyancy both underwater and at the surface as it lets you control 'where you are in the water'. Positive buoyancy at the surface means you can save energy and rest. Underwater when you are neutrally buoyant, almost weightless, you can swim effortlessly and move in any direction. Your buoyancy is controlled using your bcd and lead weights, which are worn around your waist on a belt. During your first open water dive you do a 'bouyancy' check in the water with your instructor, to determine how much weight you need. This changes as you get more when confident diving or if you change any items of your equipment.

Judith doing compass practice

I went to Tenerife with my friend Judith, whom I had done the try-dives and the open water certification with. She had chosen to do her Advanced course whilst we were there and I was pleased to see that, whilst practising for her Navigation dive, she had to walk round outside the dive school with a towel over her head to practise her 'Compass use' for the square. Interesting to note that instructors the world over use the same methods of practise – and that they find the same things amusing.

It was in Tenerife that we also used most of our 'alternative' hand signals. When we had done the try dives last year, during the instructor briefing they had shown us, jokingly we thought, a signal for 'look out there's a shark coming', and everyone had laughed as there were no sharks in Tenerife.

During our first dive this year, the instructor turned to us and gave the signal for shark, we looked at him, looked at each other and then signalled to each other about what we thought of him. Then we carried on swimming ... right up to the 2 metre Angel Shark in front of us! Learning point – there are more types of sharks than the ones seen in 'Jaws' and there are obviously some in Tenerife! We took solace in the fact that he had no idea what our signals meant and we just looked at him and enthusiastically signalled "Nice shark, thanks!"

(DPV's) Diver Propulsion Vehicles (February 2005)

This consisted of two dives with the scooters and learning how to maintain them, put batteries in etc. There was no manual to read and no knowledge reviews as the dive school didn't have them. The scooters themselves were fine, really good fun and made diving easy, although it was scary how fast you can get to depth. The first dive wasn't too bad, 20m with no stops.

However on the second dive, we went to 32m, without any weight, which first became a problem when I was trying to equalize, I couldn't do the usual pinch your nose and blow method as I started to ascend every time I took my hand off the scooter! When we reached 32m the instructor signalled for us to put the scooters down, we were going for a swim! I found this a bit scary as I had no weight on and I didn't want an uncontrolled ascent from that depth!

> **The air spaces in your ears are very sensitive to increasing pressure but can be equalized quite easily by pinching your nose and gently blowing against it with your mouth closed. This enables air to go direct from your throat into your sinus air spaces and your ears. Another technique to use is swallowing and wiggling your jaw from side to side. You are taught to equalize every few feet as you descend before they start to become uncomfortable, if you can't equalize your ears you have to discontinue the dive as continuing may result in a ruptured ear drum.**

At the end of the dive I missed my safety stop due to my lack of weight, despite numerous attempts I just couldn't stay down, no matter how much I used my lungs! I raised the issue of weight the instructor again after the dive but was told to use my lungs and grab hold of something at the end of the dive for the safety stop – great advice, I felt so much better – not!!

We did a third scooter dive, which was to be credited to my deep speciality, all the other instructors at the dive school told me I should insist on doing a buoyancy check so I could be correctly weighted weight to avoid missing my safety stop again. I tried, as did the other student but we still got no weight. As the instructor was leading the dive we also had no control over how deep we were to go, we were at his mercy!

This time we went even deeper – 36m and again stopped for a swim around which wasn't much fun as I daren't breathe in too much! I tried hard to remember what Dave had taught me when I did my deep advanced dive and I couldn't help but wish he was there, fin pivots, mask skills and all! However the fact that I had been so thoroughly trained meant that although I was a little anxious (which is never a bad thing) I was aware of what could happen and what I should do about it, this showed how important the training is in 'real life' situations.

It wasn't a good dive though and I was so glad when it ended, I managed my safety stop this time by hanging onto a rock, the other student was hanging upside down off his DPV!

Underwater Naturalist (February 2005)

Nobody was more surprised than me to get this speciality, not because it was hard but because I actually wanted to do the Fish ID Speciality! How did that happen? Well, I'm not really sure myself, I booked the Fish ID speciality with the dive school in Tenerife. I did dive number one with the required skills for the Fish ID (I checked later in the book), then I did dive number two with a different instructor, we did the de-brief after the dive and he signed my pic card and gave me a temporary card which said 'Underwater Naturalist'!! Your guess is as good as mine!! It didn't seem appropriate at that point to ask what happened to the Fish ID speciality! Another mental note: when doing dive courses abroad, check you and your instructor are both on the same planet!

Deep (February 2005)

Four dives were required for this one. They could credit the one I had done as part of my advanced as Dave had completed and signed the Advanced Diving section of my logbook (well done Dave).

I had also already done a 24m dive whilst in Tenerife as a part of a group, and as an instructor was present this was also credited, as was the third dive I did with the scooter. This left me only needing to do one more deep dive for the speciality. However after my experience on the previous dive to 36m I was very reluctant to do another deep dive.

Because of this I told my instructor that I wanted to go to just over 18m (PADI classes anything over 18m as 'deep'), for about 20 minutes. In other words I just wanted to do what I had to for the speciality certification.

The dive was fine but we went to 24m for 45 minutes, he just completely ignored everything I'd said!

This guy was starting to make Dave Small look like the saint of instructors, thank God they're not all the same!

Underwater Navigation (April 2005)

Now, you might be wondering why someone who can't navigate, and has a deep psychological fear of the compass chose to do a Navigation Speciality.

Well, all the diving I had done since becoming certified had, in some way or another, required navigation skills, whether it was a reciprocal heading back to the exit, going from one attraction to the other at Capernwray or navigating to a particular place or reef. I had also bought a very nice, brand new, top of the range compass which was hanging from my BCD (where else?) but I still couldn't navigate, and was therefore always relying on my buddy.

I had two choices, either give up trying for good and forever rely on my buddy to navigate, or have one last go at trying to learn it.

I chose the latter as I really do want to be a self sufficient diver and, there's always a chance, especially when diving abroad that I might get a buddy who was worse at navigating than me.

So, back to Fins to book the Navigation Speciality, with manual, as I needed all the help I could get. I left it to the shop to tell Dave I'd booked it – I was lying low on this one!

The 'Underwater Navigation Speciality' course teaches you to know where you are in the water and where you're going. You learn all about underwater navigation procedures, techniques, planning, organization and potential problems. You are also introduced to natural navigation, underwater patterns, distance estimation and learn how to further your compass navigation skills. The course is taught using a manual with knowledge reviews to be completed and 3 open water dives.

I knew that it was now time to come clean about my lack of compass and navigation skills and of my complete lack of understanding for the subject. I confessed all to Dave who, from my open water and advanced dives had kind of worked it out for himself – can't think how! Fortunately, he took my fears and concerns on board, without passing judgment and decided to teach me the course in a slightly different way.

We started with a classroom session, based on the information in his instructor manual, this gave me the opportunity to ask questions and to keep asking them until I understood it.

Once I understood how to use the compass properly I could practice, and I did, on the park! Everytime I took the dog for a walk I took my compass and did a square or triangle, this wasn't a problem as there's loads of odd people on my local park anyway – I didn't look out of place!

After going through the manual and doing the knowledge reviews I was ready, kind of, for the dives. Back to Capernwray!

As I now understood how to use my compass, we agreed it would be better if I did all the 3 dives required, repeating the one I had already done (unsuccessfully) for my advanced. During the briefing Dave explained that, as we were doing 3 dives we would have only the minimum surface interval between dives 1 & 2. I was okay with this – okay that was until he asked me to find the minimum surface interval required. What?! That wasn't on the skill list!! I knew I had to use my RDP (Recreational Dive Planner) but I didn't have a clue how to use it to find the minimum surface interval. As Dave went off somewhere I asked the DM for the answer and, he wouldn't give it me (thanks Chris!).

Common sense told me that if Dave had said we were going back in the water for dive 2 quickly then the required surface interval couldn't be very long. So, I tried to wing it, and when he came back I quite confidently said "8 minutes", thinking he wouldn't have the time to look it up. Did he accept my answer? Did he hell, he just said "fine, now show me how you got the answer!" – Uh Oh! There's always one!! I conceded defeat and he showed me how to find it – again, and the correct answer was 'nil' – well I wasn't far off!

Onto the dives, and the skills for the first one included the straight line and reciprocal using natural and compass navigation, I had no problem with these. Then came the dreaded square. Dave marked an X on the rock next to us and I had to navigate the square, bringing us back to that rock.

I set off quite confidently, and then realised that I should have been measuring the distance for my square to have equal sides – too late! I just went a bit further, stopped, turned and set off again, I tried to guess when I had swum

Compass practice on the park

about the same distance and turned again, it was at this point I realised the implications of not 'measuring the distance' – I didn't know how far to swim before doing the last turn to put me on the same line as the rock I had to get back too! Hmm … I did the last turn and swam a little way, I could see a rock ahead and I swam towards it thinking "please let this be the right rock". I also thought that if this wasn't the right rock, I would just draw an X on it anyway and pretend – hopefully before Dave saw me! But, I didn't need to, the rock had an X on it, I had successfully navigated the square (ish) and returned to the start point, I don't know who was more surprised, me or Dave!

We also had a repeat of the natural navigation 'take us home' skill, this time at least I knew what he meant and I navigated us successfully back to the exit!

We got out of the water, for the minimum surface interval, swopped cylinders over quickly and went back in for dive number 2. This time I had to navigate us to 5 different 'underwater attractions' that I had earlier found, and written the bearings for on my slate. Believe it or not (and I'm still struggling to) I found all 5 first time, I used my compass and navigated my way to all of them! When we got out of the water I was on cloud nine – I could navigate. I was well chuffed!!

For dive 3, Dave was to give me 4 or 5 bearings one at a time and I had to take us too them. This was going well, until we got to number 3 and Dave wrote 85 degrees on my slate, or I thought he had! I set off, from one of the boats, and guessed that I would be going to a horse. So I was confidently swimming along, maintaining my 85 degree heading, I was sure though that the horses were in the other direction – maybe I was wrong about it being a horse. Then I hit the wall, I looked at Dave who signalled 'think about it' and pointed to my compass! Now, after dives 1 & 2 I knew I could navigate, and I knew I was doing it right! I didn't know the signal though for 'I am bloody thinking about it'! So, I frowned at him, showed him my compass — 85 degrees and then showed him my slate, where he had written **185** degrees! Whoops, another slight misunderstanding! I had no problem finding the horse after that!

I then successfully did another bearing to a boat where he wrote down another heading, I remembered the skill was 4 or 5, and I'd already done 4, so I wrote on my slate 'do I have to do this one?' and he looked at me, frowned and nodded — no room for negotiation then?

After all 5 were completed, he gave me the signal to lead us back — Hey! that skill was in dive one, and I already had done it — successfully! I'd finished all my skills so I said no and signalled for him to lead us home.

Instructors, and their love of making students do skills, how frustrating can they be? He said no, so I said no again, I asked Chris, our DM and he said no, so ... I did the only thing I could ... I knelt on the bottom, crossed my arms and waited!! Another little discussion/debate, with a variety of hand signals ensued, before we all went 'home' together, well side by side really so neither of were leading or had given in.

Having passed the speciality and been given my temporary certification card, I took every opportunity to tell people about it, including by e-mail to all club members, most of them didn't know who I was, but I didn't mind I just wanted to tell everyone. I was so pleased to have 'conquered' my Navigation phobia and to discover that it can be fun. I always knew, deep down that it wasn't difficult and that there was no reason I shouldn't be able to do it, but the more I tried and failed the worse I felt about it. In the end, I feel that what made the difference was Dave 'tailoring' the speciality course to meet my needs, had it been delivered in the usual way, by just doing the dives, I know I wouldn't have grasped it!

The Navigation was also my fifth speciality. This made it even more important as I now had the 5 needed for my MSD – I was another step nearer my goal!

In between my Navigation specialty and the Rescue diver course I did some pleasure dives. One of these was at Eccleston Delph Dive site, a disused quarry near Preston. Like Capernwray it has a number of 'Underwater attractions' including a van, boat, armoured car, sports car etc. Some of which are easier to find than others. There were 6 of us diving, 3 buddy pairs – Dave and Dan, Pete and Kevin, Karen and Myself. Dan had hired his kit from Fins and so was wearing a 'student hood', which was, you guessed it, bright yellow! I could laugh as I now had my own black one! On the first dive we descended onto the Van which was marked with a rope line and then had a look round the armoured car, well Karen and I had a look round, the 4 'boys' had to 'investigate' every bit of it including sticking their heads in the door, windows etc. We then moved onto the boat where we had a look round and again the 'boys' had to look around it, swim through it and pretend to sit on the deck and drink cocktails!!

Dave was leading the dive and we then set off to try and find the sports car, one of the harder to find attractions. When he found it he indicated to show us he'd found it and we could tell how pleased he was – so I swam over and I sarcastically gave him a handclap, as he had done a thousand times during my training whenever I had successfully done a skill. He saw the funny side and we both had a good laugh, which then made my mask fill up with water, luckily I knew how to clear it – I should do I'd practised it often enough! We then had a look round the sports car, with the boys having to sit in it, pretend to drive etc. After 5 minutes or so, I signalled to Karen to come over to me and I wrote in the silt on the cars bonnet "Boys and their Toys??". It was a fun dive, which we all enjoyed, and we knew most of the attractions intimately

Guess which one is Dan

by the time we'd finished it – well, our male dive buddys did anyway!

Another pleasure dive I did was to Waswater, in the Lake District. This is a popular place for deep diving as the lake is about 65 metres at it's deepest. Although this was a pleasure dive and there was only Dave and I diving he still went through everything as if he was my instructor, dive site orientation, entry and exit points, Health and safety stuff etc. I appreciated this as I knew Waswater would be a more 'challenging' dive, and I still didn't consider myself to be an experienced diver.

As we were doing a deep dive, and I didn't have my own torch I hired one from Fins, as I knew it would be dark.

Dave had said there were no facilities there and he wasn't kidding, there was nothing, not even a tree! Thank goodness we had stopped at the garage on our way here!

I tried not to think about this as we got kitted up, it was a bit cold, damp and blustery and this made the lake and mountain at the side of it look even more scary. I got my torch out, checked I knew how it worked, took the lock off and asked Dave where was the best place to put it – stupid question, he said "hang it on your BCD" where else?

Just walking down to waters edge was a feat in itself as the ground was wet and slippery and, running true to form, I fell on my bottom at least once.

In the water it was fine, we descended and swam to about 16 metres before going over the edge of a wall and dropping down to around 40 metres. It was whilst descending that it started to get very dark, very quickly, so I went to switch my torch on. I took the lock off and tried to switch it on, it must have been the effects of the nitrogen because as you remember I had already taken the lock off before I got into the water. So ... there I was going from 20 to 40 metres in complete darkness and wondering why the hell I couldn't switch my bloody torch on! I wasn't unduly worried though as I could see the light from Dave's torch in front of me and I couldn't see my computer so I didn't actually know how deep we were. I finally realised what the problem was, took the lock off and switched the torch on just as Dave turned round and signalled 'are you OK?', so I signalled back 'OK' like the torch had been on all the time – cool diver!

The effect of nitrogen on your body changes as you breathe it under pressure. At depths approaching 30 metres, nitrogen has a noticeable, intoxicating effect that can intensify the deeper you go. A diver that is suffering the effects of nitrogen narcosis behaves like you might expect someone who is drunk to behave. It impairs the divers judgement and co-ordination and may create a false sense of security, disregard for safety and other foolish behaviour. It can also make a diver feel anxious or uncomfortable which could then lead to panic or poor decision making.

Rescue Diver (April 2005)

After reading the literature on this course, which said that it would help me to "look after myself and others whilst diving", and checking there were no mask skills or fin pivots, I decided that as a self sufficient diver, it would be a useful course to do. I also hold the first aid at work certificate and, as a nominated first aider for the organisation I work in, I have put it into practice on many an occasion. It therefore made sense to me, to extend my first aid knowledge to cover diving related incidents as well.

> **The PADI Rescue Diver course, through the combination of manual, knowledge reviews, exam, video and hands on training, teaches you the importance of emergency management and prevention. The home study materials cover the principles and information that is necessary to prevent and handle dive emergencies. During the open water dives you learn to apply the techniques in simulated, hands-on rescue scenario's. The rescue diver course builds your confidence as a diver and gives you valuable experience in emergency management and prevention. It also helps to heighten your awareness of the surrounding environment.**

Having booked the course in February I worked my way through the manual and knowledge reviews fairly quickly as I knew I had the Navigation speciality ones to do as well.

I handed the knowledge reviews into the shop as soon as I had done them, about 2 months early, so they could go in my file. I think I should have got brownie points for that!

Nothing happened then (apart from me passing my Navigation Speciality!) until the video session at the beginning of April. This was a chance to watch the PADI video, see who else was on the course, who our buddy would be (mine was to be Steve) and our DM (ours was Karen) and complete the necessary paperwork.

I found the video really useful as it helped me to 'visualize' some of the stuff in the book, and gave me more details on the skills we would have to complete, and be assessed on during the actual open water dives.

We also had chocolate biscuits and went to the pub afterwards which always helps! (I was right, divers are fickle)

Next up was the exam, on the 28th April. The evening was facilitated by Fins Instructors Ivan, Ken and Dave, who for some reason had taken on the personalities of victorian schoolteachers! No chocolate biscuits and strict exam conditions – Huh! Like we would even think about cheating!

We all passed the exam, with some very high marks and then had a useful discussion looking at the questions we had got wrong, arrangements for the weekend etc and then we went to the pub to celebrate.

Then came the open water dives ...

Day 1, was on a Bank Holiday Saturday at Capernwray. There were 8 'students', 4 Instructors and 4 DMs or Assistant Instructors. We had already been forewarned by the Instructors that, if it was very busy, we would not dive there and instead would look elsewhere. Fortunately it wasn't too bad and so we were all briefed and got kitted up.

We did 6 skills on that first day, which were; tired diver tow, panicked diver at surface, response from shore to conscious victim, distressed diver underwater, missing diver and surfacing the unconscious diver. All the skills were demonstrated by an instructor to the whole group and we then did them in our own buddy pairs.

It was busy, tiring day and in parts involved a lot of hanging around in the water and getting cold!

As well as the above 6 skills however, other useful things were learned during the day. Things such as:- a dry suit on it's own is very buoyant, you can go in the water wearing only your suit and you float really well – I actually knew this from the dry suit orientation of my first open water dive, but I'd forgotten (too much to remember), and I probably couldn't see why I'd ever do it in real life. Well, I now know why – that I might be required to go in, wearing just my dry suit, to assist a tired diver near to the shore or exit point.

Additional learning point number two was that if you stand up in the water (wearing only your dry suit) then your bottom half gets squeezed, which can lead to cramp in your legs, and all the air is squeezed into your top half

Great buoyancy – only in my drysuit!

so that's very buoyant – odd! But then I always knew dry suits were a bit odd anyway!

I also learned that throwing a rope to someone in the water, even though you are stood on the shore, is not as easy as it looks, but then how often in our everyday lives do we throw ropes to people? All the more reason to practice – I might take a rope with me to the park when I walk the dog in future – well, I don't need the compass practice now! The last learning point of the day was that all good rescue or search plans can go to pot – well, not completely to pot obviously, but unless you know the underwater topography of an area really well, plans made on the surface may need to be changed when you're underwater. Fortunately Steve and I made up a whole new set of underwater signals, when looking for the 'lost diver', to reflect this – self sufficient divers! We didn't find the missing diver by the way, and the instructors pointed out to us that if this was real life someone could be in serious trouble – mega guilt trip! Then we found out that the 'missing diver' was a milk carton attached to a concrete block – guilt trip not so mega anymore!!

Onto Day 2, Bank Holiday Sunday, which was held at Devil's Bridge in Kirby Lonsdale, a very pretty picnic site on the River Lune which is popular with bikers and divers a well as the general public.

To go to Devil's Bridge was both exciting and scary as many of us hadn't dived there before. However we trusted the Instructors (even more scary than Devil's Bridge) and knew that they wouldn't take us anywhere unsafe.

We had a number of skills to do on the day which would culminate in rescue scenarios, bringing together everything we had learned during the whole course.

First we had to practice giving an unconscious victim rescue breaths whilst getting them out of the water. Dave demonstrated on Ivan, some of the ways to lift and get people out of shallow water, managing to make them look quite straightforward and easy. However they were not easy, and the different lifts, combined with slippery rocks at the edge meant that most of us, on more than one occasion, landed on our bums and, many other parts of our body for that matter! How come Dave didn't do that when he demonstrated?

We 'gathered' numerous bruises during the day as we practised getting people out of the water, always putting our 'unconscious victim' before our pride − very commendable − and we assume (or would hope), just like real life! It was during this exercise that many of us also learned a couple of additional things − like the fact that it's nearly impossible to get your pocket mask out of your bcd pocket in a hurry and, when you do the 'valve' promptly falls out and is lost in the water!

During the lunch break we practiced CPR and administering oxygen on the Rhesus Annie doll/dummy.

As we were finishing that, and our lunch, all hell broke loose (for the first time) when Ken 'spotted' 4 unconscious divers at the surface! Great sense of timing − Yes, I know it might happen like that in real life (well maybe not 4 at the same time!) but this meant we had to run down the bank, get our fins and mask on and get into the water. This was made even more difficult by the fact that someone had mixed all the kit up, something else, they pointed out, that could happen in real life − thanks guys! But hey − when we need to, we can get our stuff on and get into the water quickly, although Pete had fastened his suit up with his wallet still in his undersuit pocket and I'd zipped mine up with my plastic slate inside, we were uncomfortable but, at least we'd put the 'unconscious' divers first and we got all them all out safely.

We then had the missing diver scenario where we had to search for, surface and assist out of the water our 'unconscious diver' (Karen). Steve and I did really well at this and found Karen quite quickly, Steve lifted her to the surface whilst I surfaced ahead of him and got my pocket mask ready (minus it's valve!). We brought her to shallow water, administering rescue breaths all the time. As we got to the waters edge we took her scuba unit off (mental note about the importance of 'Releases' on buddy checks!) and then Steve and I removed ours to make getting out of the water easier. This meant that after the exercise we had to put it back on again, in the water. Flashback: to open water certification dives and me whingeing about the 'removing and replacing scuba gear at surface' skill at Capernwray – back it was to haunt me again!!

When we got to the waters edge I asked Steve if he thought it was shallow enough for me to administer CPR, I could see that Karen was willing us to say yes as we'd already dragged her over loads of rocks – he looked at the rocks behind him and said, with a wry grin on his face, 'No, I think we need to be shallower', so we dragged her back a bit further! Well, we had been told to do it as if it was for real!

After this we were all stood around trying to get our breath back and Ken said we should start to take our kit apart and carry the cylinders up separately to the river bank. I was a bit puzzled at this as I thought we had another scenario to do, and I hadn't used my 'Accident management work slate (the bit of plastic) at all during the course so far! I asked if we'd finished and Ken, Dave and Shrek all said (with a far too innocent look on their faces) 'Yes, we've finished' so, like a fool I believed them and starting to take my cylinder off.

About 2 minutes later a 'diver' popped up out of the water, shouting 'Help, I've lost my buddy!' – Bugger! All hell broke loose again! Obviously this was the last scenario – the management of a rescue situation!

Everyone immediately started running round like headless chickens getting their kit back together and starting to put it on. As mine was completely taken apart,

Pete with wallet still zipped inside dry suit!

I knew I would never be able to put it back together quick enough to save someone (that's my excuse anyway) so, I took on the role, along with Steve (obviously he was thinking the same) of 'co-ordinating' the rescue! Actually it was more like co-ordination of Billy Smarts Circus, but we were all trying hard.

I thought all the students were superb, spotters were assigned to look for bubbles, the 'buddy' was asked relevant questions about where the diver might be lost and given appropriate first aid, divers went in to search (apart from one, who had forgot their weight belt − her heart was underwater looking for the lost diver − her body however was still on the surface) and snorkellers looked on the surface. The missing diver was found and Steve and I started first aid on the diver. So far so good, slight chaos but the missing diver was safe and all was going well − well, that is until the spotters said that they had seen 2 sets of bubbles so there must be another missing diver!! This had Sarah and Jayne frantically donning their kit and getting into the water − go girls! I think Ken and Dave stopped them just before they went in as they knew there was no other missing diver.

All in all it was an excellent course and we had all passed, but more importantly, had learned a great deal. I hope we never have to use the rescue skills we learnt on the course but if we did, other divers can rest assured that, even though we may look like headless chickens, we are actually very highly trained chickens − sorry, rescue divers!!

This was also the first course on which I had never said to Dave "why do we have to do this? why can't you help me? I'm never going to use this skill in real life"! That shows you how much I've learned − I've obviously learned (the hard way) when it's best to keep quiet!

After the course we went to the pub (obviously) where the Instructors presented us with our temporary certification cards, this was really nice and made me feel quite proud of becoming a Rescue Diver.

The last dive of the course was also my 50th dive. As I already had 5 speciality certifications and was now a Rescue diver as well, this meant ... I was a Master Scuba Diver, **and had achieved my goal of going from 'Numpty Diver' to 'MSD' in 6 months!!**

So the 'Journey' ends, I can now dive and, as you can see, I had great fun along the way.

Why did I decide to write about it? Well, a part of me wanted to share with you some of the fun I'd had but another part of me also wanted new divers to be able to read this and think ..."If she can do it — so can I!" because they'd be right! But the real reason I wrote it was ... because Dave suggested it, and, at the time, it seemed like a good idea!

So, is that really the end of the journey? I don't think so! I know I still have a lot to learn and I don't think any diver should ever be arrogant enough to think they know it all, so I will be having a good think, in the pub obviously, about my next goal.

Ten (really useful) things your instructor doesn't tell you:

1. Money – once you take up diving you never have any. Actually the instructors usually do tell you that, what they don't tell you is why you'll never have any money – because of the amount of beer you will have to buy them at the 'mandatory de-brief' sessions in the pub, or because of the million and one courses there are to do after your open water certification!

2. Fin Pivots, Hovers and Mask Skills – whatever the course, guaranteed it will have one or more of these in it. Tip: if you're writing a diving course, throw in a fin pivot, you can't go wrong!

3. Snot – On occasions, you will ascend, get out the water, take your mask off and have a face full of it! If you're lucky someone will tell you, but usually, they don't. This is what being a self sufficient diver is really all about.

4. Everything hangs off your BCD – whatever you buy, whatever it's use – if you ask the question 'where do I put this?' the answer is always the same –'clip it onto your BCD' – how much stuff can one bcd take before you start to look like a xmas tree?? And, if everything is meant to be clipped to your bcd, why do they only have two rings on them to attach things too?

5. Dry suits – yes, we nearly all learn to love them eventually but it would be nice to know from day one that they have a mind of their own!

6. Swearing – you can swear quite adequately with your regulator in your mouth. This is particularly useful to know when doing Mask skills and/or fin pivots!

7. When doing mask skills, like taking it off underwater, your hair **will** get caught in the mask making it even more difficult to take off and put back on. The instructors assure you that your hair won't get caught but then, they've all got 'divers haircuts' (skinheads) so how would they know?

8. Buying your instructor breakfast is not a skill requirement of any PADI course!

9. Every 'why' question you ask them has the same answer – because it will make you a 'self sufficient diver' Yeah but come on, buying breakfast??

10. When they say 'Slightly Refreshing' they mean 'Bloody Cold'! Unfortunately you usually work this one out for yourself – on your first UK dive!

Judith with hair caught in mask – again!

Acknowledgements

My grateful thanks go to the following people for their help, support and encouragement over the last 6 months:

- Dave Small – without whose excellent training and endless amounts of patience this would not have been possible – or half as much fun! And without whom I would still be a 'Numpty Diver'.

- Natalie Close – for always managing to look interested when I talked about diving or when I bought another piece of equipment (to hang on my BCD). For going through my knowledge reviews with me – every time I had an exam, and for never mind yet another 'chippy tea' when I'd been out diving.

- Judith Wright – for being the best open water training buddy a diver could ask for.

- Derek and Barbara Sergeant (my mum and dad) – for their continued support, text messages (to their 'little mermaid') after every dive, and good luck messages before every exam and course.

- Laura Wright – for not wanting to dive on holiday and so being able to watch our bags, keys, get drinks, order lunch, help us out of our wetsuits etc. A vital member of any dive group!

- Donna and Ian Shaw – for listening to the details of every one of the 50 dives, and all the courses, and all the dive gear I bought and still managing to look interested even though they don't dive themselves (yet!).

- Cushla McCullough (Fins) — for making me a coffee every time I went in the shop and for helping me through the 'maze' of hiring equipment, buying gear, booking courses etc.

- Colin Scowcroft (Fins Course Director) — For his support and encouragement throughout my training, and for making sure Dave was always available for all of my courses!

- Fins Watersports Preston — all it's staff and members for their help and encouragement.

- To all the other students on the courses I did, especially the Rescue Diver course.

- Photographs courtesy of Natalie Close, Dave Small, Easy Blue World and Karen Price.

And, a special thanks to all the Instructors, Assistant Instructors and DiveMasters who have assisted on my courses, and to all the "Buddy's" (especially Pete Weir and Dave Higgins) who have dived with me over the last 6 months — especially when I couldn't navigate!

Me, when I've not been diving obviously - no snot, mask mark or dive hair!

Contact Details:

Mel Close   melanieclose@prestondisc.fsnet.co.uk

Dave Small dsmall2@btinternet.co.uk

Fins Watersports, Preston. Tel: 01772 788032
www.fins.co.uk

**"The journey of a thousand miles begins
with a single step"**
(Lao-Tsze circa 600bc)

**"The journey to MSD begins with ...
getting wet"**
(Mel Close 2005)